GW00869960

Two Ducks
in Venice

Philippa Dunn & Virginia Painter

About the authors

We're only called ducks because we're no longer chicks; we're both over 55, we've both been married our whole lives – and still are, to our original choices – we both have all sorts of children and grandchildren, and we're cousins.

Sprat is called Sprat because of the nursery rhyme 'Jack Sprat would eat no fat...' and we spent the first eight years of our lives joined at the hip, inseparable, The Little Ones. Sprat moved away when she was eight but we always kept in touch and now that our families have grown, we get to play together again, at last.

Unsurprisingly we travel very well together. We eat the same sort of food, enjoy the same amount of drink, laugh hysterically at the same (some would say unfunny) things, and mostly like to see and do the same things.

This is the first time we've been to Venice together and it was such fun, and worked so well that we decided we'd write about it to inspire and encourage other 'ducks' to give it a go.

~ 1 ~

Everyone in my world has known for years how badly I've wanted to go to Venice and so when the time was right and I'd saved enough money to have a really good time without worrying about having a dinner out or buying a frivolity, I asked Sprat if she was up for it, knowing perfectly well she would be.

Originally we were going to stay in a hotel just off St Mark's Square until I told my daughter about it and her immediate reaction was 'Mom!' (she's Canadian) How come you're not staying in an apartment? It's SO much more fun than a hotel! We did it in Rome on our honeymoon and if we can do it, you two can!'

A whole day of trawling the internet ended with us booking a flat in S. Zaccaria in the Castello district, apparently 10 minutes from St Mark's Square. It's worth looking at two or three sites and comparing prices because they do vary a lot. The photos of the one we chose showed two bedrooms, a nice if rather pink-looking bathroom, little kitchen and sitting/dining room. It had everything we needed and it fitted our budget perfectly, and actually worked out to almost €200 less than the hotel. We figured that even if we got breakfast at the hotel, we'd still have to eat out for lunch and dinner, whereas in the flat we could eat in every night if we wanted to. We're both foodies, both love to cook and especially love Italian food, and what fun to cook the local food with local ingredients, and having more play money to boot. Decision made. We paid half up front and were told to bring cash for the other half, to be given to Marika when she met us off the water bus in order to take us to the flat. She emailed instructions of which bus to catch and where she would meet us in Venice - none of which made any sense of course, until we were there and could see what she was talking about. So now the big question of what to take to wear, and the countdown started.

* * * * *

This adventure didn't get off to a good start. Sprat was at the airport waiting for me and I was stuck on the motorway with a very worried husband behind the wheel. Thank the Geeks for mobile phones because I could keep her appraised of our progress – or not, as the case may be – but I did know deep down that the CS (Celestial Secretariat) would never let our first sortie be spoiled by me missing the plane. I tried to remain calm and positive while Sprat made Plans B and C. Seeking advice from a charming EasyJet member of staff, she told him the problem.

'That's bad' he said, 'but there is a later plane that you could catch.'

'That's good!' said Sprat.

'It'll cost you each an extra fifty quid though, and that's bad' came the reply. This could have gone on indefinitely but just at the right moment the traffic cleared, we made it to the airport and had time for a drink before boarding. No worries.

Marco Polo airport is small but incredibly busy, and the bank of bus ticket booths are perfectly obvious when you know where to look. When Sprat and I travel, the first thing we do is put some money into the 'kitty' – say €50 to start, topping up as needed – and that pays for everything that we do together, such as bus tickets and cups of coffee. She bought the tickets and then when we got outside the airport and weren't sure which way to go to the bus – it's not very clearly signed – we followed a stream of people few of whom were speaking Italian and must therefore be tourists for Venice. They turned left down the walkway, left again past the car park and there was the bus stop, just like any other in the world, only these buses tie up to the floating bus shelter. All passengers have to go down into the cabin unless you're a mate of the captain in which case you can hang around on deck, it seems, and the bus – *vaporetto* – very quickly turns around and sets off back to Venice. The day we arrived was quite overcast so the water was just a darker shade of grey than the sky. In the distance was a strip of even darker grey which we guessed must be land. The waterways are defined by buoys made of three huge logs fastened together and stuck in the sea bed, and some of the buoys appear to have beacons on top of them, and some not. There are speed signs and just like on the roads, some boats keep to the speed limit and the boy racers in their smart speedboats don't. A great white, multi-windowed building appeared on the left and looked as though it was floating on the water. To the right and ahead of us were lights twinkling in the dusk and two distant towers, just visible against the darkening sky. All these things stayed elusively distant from us and it was clear we weren't heading into land, but travelling round the edge of it. Later, when we looked at the map, we saw how we had gone across the top of the island, down the east coast, round the bottom corner and along between Venezia and San Georgio to the S. Zaccaria stop, as instructed by Marika. When you get off the bus battling with your suitcase and all the other disembarking passengers, it's hard to take note of your surroundings, and I was on dry land and trying to keep up with Sprat before I really realised that I had actually set foot in Venice, at last.

Marika was there to meet us – how she and Sprat found each other among the milling hordes I don't know – but she set off at a fair clip, leaving us to follow without wasting time looking about and seeing where we were.

* * * * *

My first impression of Venice was of a very wide street or walkway, really, with the sea on one side and magnificent buildings on the other. Wide steps leading up onto bridges and removable ramps from the top of the bridge, covering half the staircase and leading back down to the street. Brilliant when you're pulling a suitcase behind you. I was disproportionately excited about crossing my first canal. And there were MILLIONS of people. Marika suddenly turned left off the Riva degli Schiavoni (the real name for the promenade we were on) and down a little alley. Without much time to take it in I saw a little restaurant and one or two shops and then we came out into the most beautiful *campo*, the only details I took in immediately being tables and chairs outside the bar, a huge tree and a magnificent well head. Marika led us across the campo, out at the diagonal corner and left into a little community of shops and bars. No time to look, we followed her down this street and then a sudden right turn into our *calle.* A few doors down she stopped and unlocked a not very promising looking door. That's the wonder of doors in Venice – none of them actually looks promising, just interesting in a ragged sort of way, but behind every single one we went through is an amazing house or courtyard or some other secret wonder. The entrance hall was bright white and very clean with a marble floor – of course – with a staircase up the left wall. At the first landing Marika unlocked a sturdy wooden door and we had arrived at our lovely little flat.

Note to self: *Rooms always look much bigger in photographs!*

Even though it was a lot smaller than we had gathered from the photos, it was lovely. Clean and bright and OURS! Marika got the rest of her rent, explained about rubbish pick-up and left, promising to be in touch again about leaving day and handing back the keys. I took the smaller room and Sprat the double by mutual consent, and I pulled open the windows and then threw open the dark green shutters and looked out onto a picture-postcard Italian street. It was narrow enough for me to throw something across it and into the window opposite – I didn't but I could have. Every window on the *calle* had dark green shutters and most had a wrought iron window box or planter holders under them. By October, which is when we were there, most of the geraniums had been taken out and ivy and a few hardy annual survivors filled the pots and boxes. On the corner of the intersecting *calle*, half way down the wall, was a little peaked roof-like structure which I couldn't really make out, so when we left the flat the next morning I went and looked at it, and it turned out to be a beautiful, weathered little angel with a roof over her head to protect her from the elements. I wondered how many hundreds of years she'd been there, watching the comings and goings of her little community.

* * * * *

We decided that on our first evening we'd give ourselves dinner out rather than go and buy ingredients and cook. We left the flat and made our way into our little community, the first business in sight being a pizza restaurant. We both agreed that as we'd been given some 'fun money', we'd do something a more adventurous than pizza on our first night, so we wandered along and came across a very nice looking restaurant with only two other diners in it. The ancient Maitre d' greeted and seated us, and we looked around at the frantically busy and chaotic décor. It was lovely. We both ordered sea bass on a bed of polenta, and a bottle of white wine to share. The two chefs were cooking behind a half wall that was opposite me and behind Sprat so I could glance up and admire them. I've always said there should be a law about so many good looking men in such a small place – the whole of Italy – and I happily concede that the young Italian women are in a league of their own too. Sadly it seems they let themselves go more quickly once they're married with children whereas the men just seem to get sexier as they get older… or is it just me that thinks this?

Anyway, good looking the cooks may be, but that's about all they had to offer. The fish and polenta hardly made it out of the starting gates for either of us – dull and tasteless and very disappointing, but the wine was fine. The pannacotta was fine too but a bit big, and it's just as well we drank the bottle between us and quite quickly because something had to help dull the shock of the bill. Wow! Still, it was our first night, a gift of money and a lesson learned.

Walking home after dinner we both felt completely safe and happy. Sure, it wasn't very far from the restaurant to the flat, but the streets were busy, shops open, bar full, and souvenir stands still blocking the way into the gift shop. We bought a few supplies at the little market – coffee, bread, milk and loo paper – and carried on home. And there's something so wonderful about turning into what is obviously a residential street and opening your own front door, disappearing through it and locking it behind you, just like a local.

* * * * *

At about 2 in the morning I woke up and wondered how I could possibly be feeling any pain if I really was paralysed, which I was sure I was. I managed to turn over and get myself out of bed and lurch to the loo trying not to bang into things in my unfamiliar surroundings which were even more muddled with sleep. Still confused and uncomprehending I made my way back into my room and sat down heavily on my bed, and the metaphorical light went on. I landed on what I would have thought was the floor it was so hard, but couldn't have been because my feet weren't up round my ears. It was my mattress. Well, it was the thing that had been put on the bed frame and covered with a sheet and blanket which some might have called a mattress but which I chose to think of more as a Slab Of Incredibly Hard Wood. I thought about my options; sleep on the sofa, try and find something else to put on the mattress, crawl in with Sprat or just suck it up and sort it in the morning. I settled on the last option, pulled my sheet and blanket back up onto the bed from the floor where they had slithered, and when I lay down I realised how cardboard-like my pillow was; I suppose I'd been so tired when I went to bed that I hadn't really noticed it. I scrabbled about and tossed and turned and turned again, like a dog trying to make it's bed on the kitchen floor, and must have finally fallen asleep because when I woke up I was once again paralysed and in pain. I got up and made tea and Sprat called from her room so I made hers too and we discussed the night horrors. I'm happy to say Sprat's bed was proper and fit for human use and we discussed swapping rooms. Not yet, I said, I'll see if I can sort it out somehow. Anyway, there's a lot to be said for a good early start, enforced or not, and soon we were out of the flat and on our way down to the bar for a coffee and brioche.

I felt a bit shy about using my little bit of Italian but did manage to say *due cappuccini e questi* – pointing to a lovely flaky brioche with chocolate in it. I have vowed since this trip that I'm going to be less inhibited and much braver about using what language skills I have. When you think about an Italian in England speaking English with a heavy accent and limited vocabulary, we all just wait patiently for them to say what they can and then we help them with the rest. We don't fall about laughing and pointing and saying 'Wow, bad accent!' so perhaps the French and Italians would feel the same way about an English Duck trying her best with their language.

Note to self: *Try harder with the local language. We appreciate the effort of our visitors so I'm sure they will do likewise.*

We indicated that we would go and sit outside and the very nice girl said that she would bring our coffees for us. It was sunny and warm and the street was coming slowly to life with the shop shutters being pulled up, and the people who were on their way to work stopping and having a quick coffee and pastry, standing at the bar greeting each other and then rushing off again. At one point a little male sparrow flew down onto the table looking for crumbs, as bold as you please, and then his wife joined him, they loaded up with their breakfast and flew back across the street to their nest under a door casing.

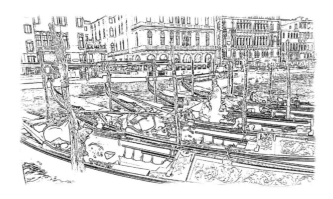

~ 2 ~

We decided over breakfast that we would find our way to St Mark's and generally get to know our little neighbourhood a bit, and get in some food. We both carried fold out maps of Venice – which we didn't really want to be seen using because it would immediately change our status from local to tourist – and once we'd located ourselves on the map, thought we'd restrict our wanderings to our side of the Grand Canal. The Great Crossing could wait. We went back to the flat, topped up the kitty, and set out again. It's all so close that you can nip home and out countless times with no effort at all. There is something so wonderful about picking your oranges – stalk and leaf still attached – and lemons, ditto, and grapes and tomatoes and having the very nice shop keeper just tally up the cost, and write it on the bag. Our little co-op market sold everything else we needed. Pasta, pesto, fresh bread, butter, cheese, wine, and chocolate. The huge pasta shells, the like of which I haven't seen in England, proved to be the perfect shape and size because they get filled up with sauce. The pesto, which we bought from the deli, was freshly made and the most intoxicating bright green; much better than a jar of pesto in every way – cheaper and fresher and completely delicious. We bought *parmigiano reggiano* cut straight from the block, as well as some *pecorino* and Dolcelatte. The gentleman in the deli was charming and patient and from then on greeted us with '*Buongiorno signore.*' I would imagine that we very quickly became The Two English Ladies – or whatever the Italian equivalent of Two Ducks might be…

* * * * *

By the time we had put our shopping away and got out again, it was getting close to lunch, or rather we were just about ready for something to eat. Luckily Sprat has a brilliant sense of direction so just setting out without any idea of where we were or how to get home didn't worry either of us.

We headed back to the seafront via the campo

we had crossed the night before. Today it was bathed in sunshine, and people were sitting on the benches and standing in little groups chatting. An elderly gentleman was escorting two old ladies in black coats, black shoes and carrying black handbags, across the campo, and the bar had set out its tables and a big closed umbrella, ready for the day. On one side of the square was a wonderful hardware shop which sold everything from glass tumblers to wellies. Next to that was an ancient house, with tall arched windows in the middle, elaborately embellished ground windows and front door over which was a huge decorated plaque which we couldn't read. We never saw anyone come or go from the house in all the time we sat at the bar opposite sipping a cold glass of wine (and feeling very local.) Next to the abandoned house was a church – San Giovanni Battista in Bragora – the bells of which rang every evening in a long peal. The church formed the corner of the square, and it joined another house with a roof garden and out of which poured numerous children to play football in the square in the evenings. Another huge house was next, and we never saw light or movement from there either. This house formed the next corner with the little street that lead down to the Riva degli Schiavoni. The first building round this corner was, although quite ragged looking, painted a beautiful terracotta colour and had baskets of plants on a balcony over the door, which had ornate mouldings around it. The plants cascaded down from the balcony to the top of the door, and almost completely covered a plaque on the wall. On either side of the door were two beautifully sculpted topiary trees. We wondered who it belonged to and ventured closer to read the plaque and found to our delight that it was the local police station. The third side of the square was occupied by a little dress shop full of beautiful, elegant clothes and shoes and bags and scarves. We looked but didn't buy. Next to this, our bar. There's nothing to make you feel so local as the barman calling out *'Buonasera signore!'* when you walk in for your evening drink. Beside and above the bar was a house with wonderful balconies on every floor. In this house lived an American family – well, American parents and completely Italian children – who were in full evidence on the last night of our stay, Halloween. Next to the bar was an alley that led to a canal, and which also ran along the side of a huge building the purpose of which we never did discover. Along the fourth side of the square was a chemist shop with the most exotic façade of wrought iron grilles and ornate windows and door embellishments. The building was filthy with age but the shopkeeper brightened it all up with little pots of ferns outside the front door. And finally, next to that, was a very low-key hotel, we think it might have been a residential hotel because we only ever saw some elderly people coming and going, and no obviously touristy guests. We talked about the possibility of living there when we grew old(er). What would our name be on the doorbell? Ah, of course... PH for Phil, and AT for Sprat - PHAT. And that made up the heart of our little neighbourhood, which we became part of quickly and easily.

* * * * *

When we popped out of our alley on that first morning into blissfully warm sunshine and onto the *riva,* we were immediately into a different Venice. Throngs of people going in both directions, so we just plunged in and turned right and went with the crowd. At the first bridge we came to we had to stop and take a photo, of course, straight up the canal, and then we stood and marvelled. Most striking was how high the water was on the buildings; it came to within inches of the door steps. And the buildings themselves; they all had peeling plaster leaving great patches of exposed brick like sores on a skin. The grilles on the windows were rusty and peeling and the doors looked as though they would no longer open. And yet, falling down as it is, Venice is inhabited and bustling and still very much alive. It actually looks exactly like all the pictures in the brochures and the paintings, but they don't show how ragged it is all becoming; for all that, it's one of the most atmospheric and captivating places I've ever been. So far – half a day into our adventure – it had lived up to everything I had hoped for. The other thing that amazed me the whole time we were in Venice was the colour of the canal water. I had heard so much about how dirty the water is: fall in and don't worry if you can't swim because you'll die from the filth first. But it wasn't like that at all. The canals were, mostly, a lovely greeny-grey colour, completely free of litter and rubbish as far as I could see, and absolutely no smell at all. I'm sure the stories of the filth were, at some time, quite true, but Venice is impressively clean. Rubbish pick-up is regular; a man with a handcart goes around the streets early, scooping up the bags. It all sounds rather medieval, but nowadays his cart is aluminium and light-weight and his uniform has high-viz stripes, and I'm impressed by the discovery that Venice recycles all its rubbish in a huge plant outside the city. All the waste is collected and processed into pellets which are then used as fuel in the power station. Such a brilliant solution when there is obviously no room for a land fill and dumping at sea is not an option.

Without hurrying we arrived at St Mark's square, only vaguely aware that we had passed the famous Danieli Hotel, the Doge's Palace, crossed the Ponte della Paglia, passed the Bridge Of Sighs, and La Pieta, Vivaldi's church and music venue. All in the tiny distance from our flat. Intoxicating.

* * * * *

The closer we got to St Mark's Square the more we battled with the crowds of people. I had been advised by a friend, a regular visitor to Venice, to get up really early one morning and come down to St Mark's before the crowds turn out, so Sprat and I didn't really worry about not being able to get near anything because we had a secret Plan B. What I did worry about was losing Sprat, and falling foul of a pickpocket, in that order. As we crossed the square, I kept talking to Sprat and discovered, when I turned round, that a foreigner was looking at me rather nervously wondering whether they were expected to reply or not, and Sprat was two steps behind me on the other side, looking up at something wonderful and not listening to me anyway. Everyone's done it but it gets no less embarrassing. We made it across the square and even got a couple of photos, and arrived at the other side without losing each other or any possessions. A good morning so far. We had reached the Holy Grail that is St Mark's church, and were interested to see that the queue of people waiting to go into the church were standing on raised platforms that snaked round from the side of the building to the front door. Under the platforms there were substantial puddles from which the platforms were saving the pilgrims' shoes. I supposed – correctly – that this was because of *aqua alta,* which can of course start at any time but is most usual in November. I was weirdly excited at the prospect of experiencing this phenomenon and wasn't even too worried about getting my new Venice shoes wet. In fact we only saw signs of it once more in the week we were there, but the locals obviously knew something we didn't, because seeing people at work in their wonderful Italian couture clothes, and wellies, became quite commonplace.

It's hard to talk and marvel and laugh when you're both battling to keep moving forward and not lose sight of each other, so Sprat and I decided it was time to find somewhere to eat and talk about what to do next. We headed out of the square and then had the task of deciding whether we wanted a bar and *panini,* or a coffee shop or a proper restaurant, but really it didn't take long to make the decision.... so we found what looked like a promising little bar and dived in. We found a table near the back which was being vacated at the perfect moment and then we figured out that we had to go and choose our food and drink and bring it back to our table with us. Stacked behind the glass counter were so many combinations of bread and buns and meat and veg and cheeses that it was nearly impossible to decide, but we both reckon you can't go wrong if you love that sort of food anyway, so we just closed our eyes and pointed. A glass of white wine each is easy to order and off we went to our corner, so proud of being so local!

Between mouthfuls of delectable bread and meat and sips of bottled ambrosia, I said

'Is this great or is this really great?'

'This is *really* great.'

'Mmm, thought so.'

Just at that moment there was a bit of a commotion round the door and in walked two gondoliers in their straw hats with red ribbons, striped jerseys (cashmere, I expect), and tight black trousers. They were obviously well-known because their drinks appeared with their plates of food, amid a lot of talking and laughing and no obvious decision making. I really wanted to get a photo of this living epitome of Venice but realised we'd be rumbled as tourists the moment I produced my camera, which would never do. So I did the old subtle pretend-to- look-at-the-time-on-your-iphone-but-really-you're-taking-a-photo thing, the result of which is over exposed and not very sharp but it's the back view of a real gondolier, nonetheless. In hindsight I wondered why this was such an event considering that we could walk ten feet past the bar and take as many photos as we liked of the gondoliers doing their thing in their proper work environment, but I suppose it's because we caught them off duty and out of Tour Operator mode that it seemed a bit more exciting and authentic. Doesn't take much...

* * * * *

After lunch we decided we'd head back to the flat and even though we weren't really sure how to get there, we both had a vague idea of the direction and folded maps if needed. Everything about Venice is unlike anywhere I've ever been before. The streets are narrow and the buildings all more than one storey, of course, because so many people had to live in such a tiny space. Now I expect many of the houses are empty. It seemed to us that you could wander along these narrow, quite dark lanes, and then suddenly pop out into a *campo*, full of sun and people and always a wonderful well-head and generally a tree or two. You come across canals unexpectedly too. You move from shop to shop looking longingly in the windows and suddenly find yourself climbing a set of steps up to a bridge. And the shops are quite different too. I suppose there must be supermarket chains somewhere, and hardware and shoe and clothing chain stores, but all we saw were small, individual shops selling the most amazing and uncommon things. On a busy canal street was a wonderful shop selling silk tassels, braids and brocades and velvet and tapestry – everything required for a grand *palazzo* – and just round the corner a shop selling cheap and cheerful Venice mementos. Across the canal, in a tall building with an elaborate marble facade was the factory outlet for a lace maker on the island of Burano. And no tourist town would be complete without its knock-off vendors who quite blatantly set up shop right beside the real deal. One shop selling beautiful hand-tooled leather bags and purses was right beside a shop selling what appeared to be the same items, only they were a third of the price and no comparison in quality. A fishmonger with an open fronted shop in which he had displayed a wonderful selection of fish and prawns and octopus on a bed of ice, was right opposite a shoe shop. We were just far enough away from St Mark's and off the beaten track to have these little streets almost to ourselves, no pushing and shoving, and then occasionally we'd have to press against the wall to let a guided group of tourists go by with their cameras round their necks, jumpers round their waists and the constant worry of what their next meal would be and where.

We did try and take note of some of the shops in relation to the canals but over the week we discovered a funny thing; the streets in Venice move. I'm absolutely convinced of it. On our way home the first day we arrived in a square the prominent feature of which was the church of St Zaccaria. Huge and magnificent outside and so probably just as amazing inside. We took the required photo and promised ourselves we'd come back in the week and go into the church. It sounds completely feeble, I know, but we only found the church twice more; once by chance and once deliberately, after a LOT of walking, only to find it was shut. We never just happened upon it again even though I swear we passed the same shops, recognised where we were, headed the way we knew we should and still we couldn't find this enormous church again. Very strange, very Venice.

We came down off a bridge, crossed a little square to the *calle* leading out of it, and Sprat said

'Here we are.'

'Where are we?'

'We're at home,' she said. 'See? That's our pizza restaurant and our bakery.' Amazing. To get

24

home we turned left by the bakery shop and had a look in the window. Not a lot left, of course, because we were so late but we did buy ourselves a divine little tart with almonds on top.

Note to self: *If you want to buy fresh, shop early. What is on display is all there is - no more in the back like the supermarkets.*

* * * * *

We're both quite keen on the idea of a siesta, especially when on holiday, but before I could rest my weary legs I had to sort out my bed. I rummaged about in the cupboards and found a huge, thick duvet which I folded into three and put on the Slab Of Hard Wood under my sheet. I folded a thinner quilt into about the size of a pillow and put it over my Cardboard Headrest, then I lay down and was pleasantly surprised; 'this will work!' I thought. I hadn't factored in how different it is to try it when you're wide awake, and to wake up after four hours of unmoving sleep. That discovery would wait. A little reading and a gentle snore soon put us right and after a cuppa, we headed out to explore our local shops before supper, and discovered all sorts of surprises. A fishmonger with a most elaborate grille over the front of the shop, the top half of which was open, and the bottom half of which was covered with a heavy board. On the board were decals of leaping dolphins... Further on was a clothes shop which must have relied entirely on repeat customers because it was so small and so far off the beaten track, I can't imagine any tourists finding it. Beside the clothes shop was our breakfast bar and opposite that our excellent little market and a dry cleaners in a tiny but wonderfully elaborate building. Next, an art gallery, the owner of which we got to know a little bit and she turned out to be a fount of information and full of excellent suggestions for visitors to her Venice. Then a *sale e tabacchi* – salt and tobacco – which nowadays is just a tobacconist, and was run by a pretty dodgy looking guy. Round the corner was a wine shop which we admired but didn't frequent having discovered that the wine we bought at the co-op market was excellent and a lot less pricey. So really everything we needed was right around the corner from our little flat. We wandered across the square to the bar and got ourselves a glass of wine and sat outside in the warm evening, just enjoying watching the community come home and disappear behind their doors for the night. Knowing we had another bottle waiting for us in the fridge we walked slowly home for some delicious food. Sprat cooked – she is very good, it must be said – and we savoured every mouthful of the giant pasta shells, fresh pesto sauce, cheese and fruit. It should be added here that for this whole evening not a moment had passed when we weren't talking or laughing or sighing with contentment. By the time I braved my bed I was too tired from walking and soporific from delectable food to consider the torture ahead of me.

Just before I turned out my light I called across the little hall

'Would you rather be anywhere else doing anything different?'

'Naa, can't think of anything. You?'

'Naa. 'Night.'

''Night.'

~ 3 ~

I really, really wanted to be strong and stoical about my night and my aching hips and sore back but when I took Sprat her tea and she said,

'How was your night? Any better?' all I could manage was,

'Grruummghrrghrr.'

'Right!' she said, 'tonight I'll sleep in there and you'll sleep in here.'

'No, just let me try again with more padding this time and we'll see if I'm getting more used to it. I can always come out and sleep on the sofa too, you know, so really this is quite self-inflicted.

Thanks, tho.' I did appreciate the offer but really, what a wimp I was becoming, and that's just not on. Why should she have a rubbish night anyway? She is a year older than me, after all.

It took us few mornings to figure out the coffee routine. We discovered that if you sit outside to drink your coffee and eat your warm, flaky brioche, you get charged €1 extra. We only discovered this because one morning when we had ordered and gone outside to sit in the sun and wait, another couple went into the cafe, ordered and come out to sit, just as we had. When Clara, the lovely waitress with thick curly hair and dark eyes, came out with our coffees she was most put out and told the other couple that they would have to pay extra because she had charged them to stand inside, and to eat outside at a table cost more money. My Italian isn't fluent by any means, but that was very easy to understand. I suppose we had never figured it out because we just paid for ours and went and sat down, never really paying attention to how much it was. (This is an attitude you can easily adopt when you've been saving for four years and can spend money like a rich person for a week.)

The other thing we discovered was how to get a really hot cup of coffee. For the first couple of mornings it wasn't all that hot which is a bit disappointing; the first time that happens you can shrug it off as an unusual occurrence, but when it happened for the third morning, it suddenly dawned on me.

'I know why our coffee is cold!'

'Why?'

'If you want hot coffee you have to ask for it! Everyone wants their coffee cold enough to drink on the run, don't they? They come in, order their coffee and mostly just gulp and run. In order to do that the coffee must be tepid. So, if we want to sit and enjoy it I reckon we have to specifically ask for it to be hot.'

'And do you know how to do this?' Sprat answered.

'I do - we ask for *caffe caldo.*'

'Right then, we'll try it tomorrow.'

And when tomorrow came and we ordered our coffee, I said the magic words and Clara looked at me with genuine surprise.

'Caldo?'

'Si, caldo' I said with great confidence, suddenly worried that I'd got the wrong word and our coffee would arrive with ice in it. But no, when our coffees came out they were steaming hot and utterly delicious.

The next day we didn't have to even ask; as soon as we ordered, the barrista asked rather nervously

'Caldo?'

'Si, grazi' said I, gratified by the recognition.

I suppose this had been the topic of conversation passed from one member of staff to the other, so now everyone knew that The Ducks liked their coffee hot. Excellent result.

* * * * *

Everyone knows that a visit to Murano is really a non-negotiable part of the Venice experience, and so it should be because it is all about glass which is a good deal of what Venice is all about, really. I had been a bit feeble about figuring out how to do this, but Sprat was completely confident that all we had to do was go down to the *vaporetto* stop and ask them; they must deal with millions of visitors a year asking exactly the same question and if they didn't know how to direct us they should be in another job. Sounded very reassuring and reasonable, so after we bought our groceries for supper that night, recharged our batteries with a little siesta, and set off for Murano.

There was a little confusion when we bought the tickets because we seemed to be having trouble making it clear that we wanted return tickets. We repeated this a couple of times and then when no one seems to be understanding the other it all gets a bit embarrassing so we took our tickets and waited in line for the bus. Of course it's obvious that the ticket would automatically be a return because what tourist would be requiring a one-way ticket to Murano? We didn't actually figure this out until it was time to come home.

The boat ride to Murano was wonderful. We stood outside on the deck and watched Venice slowly shrink behind us. We hadn't really tried to work out how far Murano is from Venice, thinking, I suppose, that it's all quite close and easy, but in fact it was quite a long boat ride, probably about half an hour.

The weather was wonderfully warm, the sky clear and the water only a bit choppy. If you have any doubts about what you should do when you arrive at Murano, fear not. Standing on the jetty is a member of staff from one of the huge glass producers who greets you by traffic-policing you to the factory for a glass blowing demonstration. We went along obediently and were led through the very swept-up entrance to what is obviously a big set up. To the left was the shop belonging to the factory and to the right hung a heavy curtain through which we were directed. We found ourselves in a sort of little theatre. On the right were wooden bleachers, about four high. To the left was a rope barrier behind which were two fairly elderly gents, one of whom was blowing glass and the other, obviously his assistant, fetched as directed. There were only a few others in the audience and we arrived close to the end of it all so we were ushered out again after about ten minutes. Not an auspicious start. There was only one route available to us all and that was straight across the passage and into the giant shop – naturally. The shop consisted of three fairly large rooms, each full to the ceiling with glass of every description, all displayed on glass shelves and counters. There were bowls and baskets full of mass produced glass balls and beads. Whole series of designs had their own portion of a room; some huge items – bowls and vases and plates – were displayed on the higher shelves and mass produced key rings and magnets and paper knives with glass handles, and anything else that could be made in glass, in fact, were all at eye level all around the shop. The colours were mesmerising and the quantities overwhelming, but somehow we did manage to escape without buying anything, mostly because we didn't want to buy until we'd had a proper look at what else there was on the island.

It turned out to be a good decision, because just a little way further down the promenade, we came to a small, long, narrow shop which looked less mass produced and more personal, so we decided to give it a go. We were the only customers in there so we took our time and worked our way slowly down the length of the shop to the counter at the back. Behind the counter sat a very nice looking man, who I would guess was just on the other side of retirement age but well away from retiring. It didn't take us long to get into a conversation with him. His English was excellent and his accent charming. The first lesson he gave us was about the lovely little watches that have a ring of tiny *millefiori* around their faces. I really wanted one, but had seen so many at so many different prices, that I didn't really know what I was looking at or how to make a sensible decision. Our lovely man explained that on the back of the watch,

'Here, thees place...' he said, taking one out of his shop window and trying to peel the clear label off the engraving we could see, 'must say Murano glass or it is from China and not made by anyone's hand at all.'

'And this one?' I asked, 'this is made by whose hand?'

He just managed to stop himself from snorting at my ignorance and said 'Thees ees made here, in my factory. I used to make these millefiori myself but now my boys do it.' Understandably his chest puffed out just a bit. Obviously this was the real deal, so I got one with a dark blue leather strap and the beautiful little glass beads seemed to dance round the watch face.

Now it was time to look for glasses, and Sprat

had seen some wonderfully interesting little tumblers, so thin and light and brightly coloured, which she asked him about. As he talked about the glass and about the techniques used and the history of his business – generations and generations had worked at that same place – his wonderful sense of humour began to show through with his pride in his family history and the legacy he had given to his children. I bought a beautiful little disc pendant made of the richest blue glass surrounded by the tiny millefiori again, but with the initial H painted, in gold and obviously by hand, in the middle of the disc. Two things quickly became obvious to us; the first was that there was a real danger that we would buy every single one of the presents on our lists right here and then not have any reason to spread the wealth or even to go and look at what anyone else had to offer. The other obvious thing was this here was a willing fount of information; we could ask him anything about Venice and the local customs and he would be delighted to share his knowledge, so in we dived.

'Can I ask you something?'

'Of course. What you wanto know?'

'All around Venice we have seen people drinking a bright orange drink and we wonder what it is.'

'Ah! that is a spreetz' he said. 'It is what

Venetians drink all the time.'

'And what is it exactly?' I wanted to know. I think of a '*spreetzer*' as being white wine with a dash of soda water in it to make it fizz, but this obviously had some other magic ingredient in it.

I was right, and the magic ingredient can be one of a selection of additives, Campari or Aperol, being the most usual. Aperol is very like Campari but has a lower alcohol content and is a bit more orange in colour than Campari. This discussion on spritzers led onto other alcoholic advice, one piece of which was that we could have our spritzer with Prosecco but he didn't recommend that, he thought that Prosecco should be enjoyed alone.

'And eef you don't finish your bottle of Prosecco' he paused significantly here and looked from me to Sprat and back again, 'Eef you don't finish it, then you must put a silver spoon in the top of the bottle, and that will keep the bubbles there for when you can finish drinking the bottle.'

I had never heard this theory before but when I repeated it at home, most people already knew this. Oh, I have so much to learn.

When we had finished discussing the merits of spritz and Prosecco, our friend said, 'And now, I have told you everything I know. Eef you don't know what to do after you have had your spreetz or your Prosecco, well, I cannot help you!' A high note and the perfect one for us to take our leave on. We gathered up our purchases and promised to return one day, and left.

'Who did he remind you of?' I asked Sprat.

'Don't know, who?'

'Dad.'

'Oh yes! He was so like T! I hadn't thought of that!'

'It was the informal lecture and the twinkle in his eye that did it for me.'

'No wonder we both liked him so much. Where to next?'

'Let's just walk along here, cross over that bridge maybe, and work our way back. Plan?'

'Plan.'

* * * * *

We were walking beside quite a wide canal in which there were all sorts of motor boats tied alongside. On the land side the buildings were of various sizes and heights and stages of disrepair but were, for the most part, painted in lovely ochre and terracotta and cream and cinnamon colours. Without much to indicate it, we'd suddenly come across the windows of another glass dealer. There were slight variations in the products they each offered, but in each one, almost without exception, there was a line of heavy, inelegant but beautifully coloured sets.

Tumblers, wine glasses, plates, platters, jugs etc. Stripes of bright colours - red, blue, green, purple, orange - ran vertically up the 'facets' in the glass. They were everywhere. I began to wonder how, or indeed why, all these factories would produce an identical line. We would eventually get the answer. In the meantime, we walked from shop to shop, warm in the late afternoon sun, but not inspired to buy anything at all. I wanted to buy a scent bottle and Sprat wanted beautiful Venetian wine goblets, just for starters, but nothing really inspired us, so we wandered happily along, going in and out of shops. We did take pictures of a couple of wonderful doors - huge, weathered and interesting - and of a marvellous fresco over one door. It had once consisted of three frescoes, two small on either side and one large one in the middle. They were framed in domes of beautifully carved wood over ancient wooden portcullis-like gates. One of the smaller frescoes was still intact and showed what might have been the coat of arms of the house. The middle, large fresco, was quite badly damaged, but what remained was still bright in colour and showed an elegant lady – perhaps a queen because she wore a coronet – sitting on a bench decorated with flowers and talking to what might have been a god; he had a headband with a little pair of wings attached to it, rather like Mercury on the Interflora logo. The third and very sad little fresco had been completely destroyed and its dome was being propped up with a fan of wooden batons. By the time we had crossed the bridge, marvelled at the colonnaded Basilica dei Santi Maria e Donato right by the canal, and wandered right round to the bus stop again, we were regretting not buying everything we'd wanted at our Lovely Man's shop because we hadn't seen a single thing we wanted anywhere else. We could see his shop from where we were across the canal and he'd closed up and gone home to Venice for the night, so there was no point racing back trying to make amends.

Note to self: *When you see something you love, buy it!*

* * * * *

It was at this point that we figured out the return part of the ticket. At the bus stop there are what look like little ticket machines with a screen and a scanning pad. We read the instructions which quite clearly told you to swipe your ticket so I did, the screen said something that looked as though I'd done it right so Sprat did hers too. We later discovered – by reading the DK guide, of course – that this is how you validate your tickets. There are seldom ticket collectors on the boats and travelling free is a risk that many take, but the fines are steep and the €6, or however much it cost, seemed like a better option. Another lesson learned.

As we stood on the landing stage waiting for our bus, the sun started to set behind the tower of what might have been a church but we couldn't tell whether the piece on top of the onion dome was a cross or a weather vane. No matter, the building was silhouetted perfectly in front of the ball of fire that was the sun, and the golden paths of light it shed on the water led straight towards us. We watched the sun set into the water all the way back to Venice and arrived home tired and happy and ready for a bowl of pasta and a bottle of wine. We decided that it was such a beautiful warm evening we might as well put our new-found spritz knowledge to the test first, though. At our little bar in the campo we ordered the spritz and I think we both ended up with Campari because it was quite red and not at all bright orange like the ones on the table next to us. I wasn't about to send mine back and ask for a colour adjustment so we settled with what we had and gave it a go. Hmmm. An acquired taste perhaps, but not something I'll work on any time soon. Next time we're in Venice I'll try the one with Aperol and see if it's any less ferocious. I'm relieved to say Sprat didn't enjoy it any more than

I did, so perhaps it really is a learned delight.

Cold meats, cheeses, olives, tomatoes and co-op wine very soon sorted out our battered palates and we fell into bed exhausted after another magic day.

~ 4 ~

An early start the following day was no hardship for me – the bed hadn't improved and I hadn't got more used to it – and we were out of the flat with just a cup of tea and a piece of fruit for sustenance. We were too early for our cafe, and the sun hadn't even appeared. The *riva* was a completely different place. There were hardly any people to be seen; a street cleaner, some people aiming to be at work early, and only one or two other over-eager tourists like us. There was a fog on the sea that came onto the *riva* but only part way so you could walk in mist or clear, depending on which side of the promenade you chose. The beautifully elaborate street lamps were still on, their pink glass making a soft glow in the mist around them, and St Mark's Square was all but empty. Turning back to the sea, the two columns of San Marco and San Teodoro stood silhouetted against the pale misty sky. San Teodoro – who was the patron saint of Venice before St Mark – looks as though he's standing over his hunting trophy of a crocodile, but actually it's a dragon. On the other column is the winged Lion of St Mark. Superstitious Venetians won't walk between the columns because in the 18th Century it was where criminals were executed. The top of St Mark's campanile was lost in the mist and the lights all round the square were reflected in the damp flag stones underfoot. It was quiet and rather eerie and needless to say the Basilica was still closed. I don't know why we thought we'd be able to get in that early in the morning, but it didn't really matter because this was our chance to see everything there was to see in the *piazza* without being pushed or trodden on or otherwise annoyed. We walked slowly under the arches of the Doge's Palace towards the basilica and made ourselves dizzy standing in front of the church and looking up at the facade mosaics which we thought, at first, were frescoes. I did wonder how the colours had stayed so bright but then Sprat pointed out that they were fabulous, awe inspiring mosaics. Moving to our left and looking up at the clock face of the Torre dell'Orologio I was struck by the incongruity of the zodiac signs right alongside the church. I don't know enough about that period in history to know how closely astrology and religion were linked but it did strike me as an unlikely combination of schools of thought. Interestingly, when the clock is working the figures of the Magi come out of the side doors to pay homage to the Virgin and Child whose figures are set above the clock, so clearly astrology and religion were closely linked and this wonderful and elaborate time piece, built for seafarers, is a true testament to the '...scientific progress, civic enlightenment, and Christian faith' of the Serene Republic.

* * * * *

By now we were a little damp and cold and ready for a steaming coffee and we set off in search of it. We headed towards the Rialto – the signs are many and obvious at this point – hoping in vain that we would find somewhere to warm up and get some breakfast. Before we knew it we had reached the Rialto – it's amazing how fast you can travel through the streets of Venice when there's no one in your way – which was much bigger than we had expected and which was quiet and crowd free. It looked as though its many eyes were shut and we did wonder whether these were, in fact, shop fronts which had yet to open, or whether the whole place had shut down and started going to ruin and that the bridge was now just a bridge. We stood at the top of it and looked down the Grand Canal. The mist had crept up, gently covering the slowly moving boats and the secured gondolas with a veil of the palest grey. The few boats that were moving slid smoothly and silently along. A restaurant and a hotel had their outside lights still on, but the tables were empty and there were no signs of it opening up yet, so we carried on over the bridge and headed for the market.

We were sure that, in keeping with markets all over the world, a fruit and veg market would open early to accommodate the retailers in the city, and we weren't disappointed. Boxes full of bunches of bright red little chilli peppers waiting to be unpacked; strings of enormous cloves of garlic and strings of chillies hanging on hooks over the tables which were covered in mounds of every single shape and colour of fruit and vegetables that you can imagine. A few customers – mostly elderly with a little shopping bag and a clear idea of the day's menu – were already shopping and we just walked in and started shopping like everyone else.

By noon the stall holders start packing up, so an early start was well done. We walked slowly to the end of the fruit stands and found ourselves in the fish part of the market, and marvelled at the spectacular displays of every kind of fish and lobster and crab and shrimp. It was all so fresh that there was no smell of fish at all, and looking up we saw that the columns were carved with all manner of wonderful sea creatures. All along the edge of the market were tiny shops selling baked goods, cold meats, cheeses, flowers etc, and the floors of the shops looked as though they were covered in old Lino made to look like coloured pebbles cut in half but which, in fact, turned out to be the ancient, original marble floors. Carrying fish round with us for the morning didn't seem like a very good idea, so we passed the old gent deftly peeling and slicing fresh artichokes and dropping them into a bucket of salted water – Venetian fast food – and bought ourselves some essentials like tomatoes and lemons, and headed back to the Rialto. Under the bridge we found a little shop that sold gondoliers' sweaters – cashmere of course – and they had children's outfits to match. The 'eyes' we had seen earlier were little shops and businesses, all of which were beginning to pull up their shutters and hang out their wares and ready themselves for the day. I always think of very high quality leather products as being synonymous with Italy and I wasn't disappointed now. I bought a handbag from a rather surly gentleman, but perhaps he was tired and ready for the tourist season to end so he could sleep in in the mornings until the next onslaught.

By the time we had finished shopping on the Rialto, Venice had definitely woken up. People were beginning to stream onto the bridge, and making our way back to St Mark's, we were just two of many. We decided we would have coffee when we got back to St Mark's, standing only, drink and leave so the next people can move forward to the bar. We sat on one of the duckboards drinking our coffee, confident that we wouldn't have to queue too long to get into the basilica because we were so ahead of the crowds. By the time we did get up and get going, however, we still had to stand in the queue and walk slowly down the side and round the corner of the church till it was our turn to go in. It's all fairly disorganised actually, and we ended up following the people in front of us who in fact led us right back out onto the street where we'd started from! Feeling a bit foolish we turned back and walked against the flow of exiting sightseers and found the right way into the church.

Everyone flocks to St Mark's with good reason. It is absolutely stunning, and it needs a lot of time, and preferably no grocery bags, to see it and appreciate it properly. For the rest of my life, whenever I think of St Mark's, I will think of the mosaics and all the gold. It's quite overwhelming, and every time we return to Venice I hope we'll go and spend some time in there, trying to absorb a little bit more. In an effort not to wax too lyrical, I will just say it is magnificent, it defies understanding and I feel privileged to have seen it, actually.

By the time we'd made our way round and out of St Mark's, both Sprat and I were properly ready for some sustenance. Being completely uninhibited by the bar routine, we went into the first one we liked the look of, and sat munching contentedly on our *tramezzini* and sipping our lovely cold wine.

We were both ready for a little lie down, so we went home, put away our purchases, recharged our batteries and went out again.

We had passed the art gallery near the flat several times and decided today we would go in and have a look. In the window we'd seen some charming little crosses decorated with tiny mosaics. The shop was run by a young lady called Adrianna, and her shop was called Alice in Wonderland. Because she seemed predominantly to sell mirrors with bright, exciting mosaic frames, we thought perhaps it was something to do with Alice and the looking glass, but it turned out that when she was little, Alice in Wonderland was one of her favourite stories told to her by her father who had another shop on the via Garibaldi. She was more than happy to talk about herself and Venice and to answer all our questions. One of the first that I asked her was about the seemingly mass-produced lines of glass ware that we'd seen on Murano.

'Huh!' she scoffed, 'that is all made in China! Nothing like that is made in Murano.'

'But why would they do that?' I asked.

'Because the tourists will buy it,' she said. 'Many of them don't care where it was made, just where they bought it. Proper Venetians,' she continued, 'would never buy it, and my family would never sell it in our shops.'

One thing led to another, and we started talking about what we'd been doing since we arrived in Venice, and said we still hadn't been on a gondola yet, and were a bit disappointed by how expensive they were.

'Pah!' said Adrianna, 'you don't want to go on a gondola! Terrible men, gondoliers, and the reechest men in Venice'. She waved them off, nose in the air, scorn dripping from her words, and neither of us dared ask why she was so against the gondoliers but we both had a guess over a glass of wine later that evening. She did give us an excellent idea though.

'Have you been on a traghetto?' she asked.

'Is that the boat you stand up on and go across the Grand Canal?' I had heard about this from a friend but hadn't given it a thought really.

'Yes, they are gondolas. They cost 50c and they take you across the Grand Canal. Plenty of time for you to take a picture of each other, and eh! you have your gondola ride!'

We promised her we would do it.

'Have you also been to San Georgio?' she asked.

'No, where is that?'

'It is the island that is opposite St Mark's, you must have seen it when you came into Venice.'

'Oh yes, we know it.'

'Go there,' she said, 'and you can go up the campanile for no money and you will get the best view of all of Venice. A better view even than from the campanile in St Mark's, and you don't have to stand in the line either, because no one goes there!'

We promised to do that too and quite confidently now that we had an idea of how to read the bus timetables. Happily we both bought a little mosaic cross each and I bought a beautiful tumbler for my Mum; it was made of such fine glass and was so light that Mum would have no problem lifting it with her stroke-weakened arm.

* * * * *

It was too late in the day to go to San Georgio so we decided to get some present shopping done and set off to the *riva* where all the stall holders were out in full force, as they must be all summer. Buying presents in Venice for everyone is easy and a great pleasure, especially when you have foodie recipients because there are all the exotic pastas, chocolates and of course amaretto biscuits to give them. These were going to be a challenge to pack and get home whole, but both Sprat and I succeed in our attempts and they were by far the most popular gifts. In our wanderings we came across a tiny glass shop – one of many, certainly, but with something special about it – and Sprat bought two wine glasses of the most exquisite, paper-thin glass, completely unadorned but utterly classic Venetian in design and each one a bright jewel colour ; turquoise for Sprat's husband and red for herself. The very charming shop keeper promised to ship them to Cornwall to arrive not much after Sprat got home, and true to his word they arrived intact, beautifully packed and ready for Christmas giving. We found a shop that just sold hand made calligraphy pens and letter openers. Another sold scarves and ties and pashminas made only of silk, silk velvet and cashmere. A stationery shop survived by selling hand made paper journals bound in leather, and beautiful pens and pencils, and 'school supplies' that you surely wouldn't risk taking to just any school. A shoe shop run by an ancient gent sold both silk and velvet slippers, all hand made and surprisingly affordable. While we were looking in the window he came out of his ancient little shop wearing a white coat and pushing a trolley full of bright silk slippers. At one point we found ourselves in the inevitable high-end shopping district – Chanel, Gucci and their ilk, and we both felt a bit panicked, not being high-end-shopper types.

'What are we doing here? Let's get out, quick! This isn't OUR Venice!' and I followed Sprat as she headed off and away from the place we wanted the least.

* * * * *

We crossed countless bridges, turned this way and that down the little alleys, most of the time with absolutely no clue where we were but completely undaunted and loving it all. Going down one street we saw a group of people in front of us turn into a huge doorway and when we reached it and looked in, we decided to follow. A narrow passage opened out into a beautiful courtyard on one side of which was a very modern glass swing door with a sign indicating that it led to a museum. We decided to save it for another time because it was about to close, but of course because we didn't make a note of the street and/or canal it was near, we never found it again. Walking round the little courtyard we were delighted by the tops of the wall columns that had carved baskets on the top of each one, all different. One had artichokes and corn, cabbage and grapes and the next grapes and pears and onions etc. We would never have found this little secret treasure if we hadn't been brave enough to follow the people who obviously knew where they were going, but we were also very relieved we hadn't followed invited guests into a private party!

On the way we found a tiny stationary shop with heavenly bookmarks made out of maps of Venice and little garden journals in Italian and jewel topped pencils, and having to redirect ourselves only gave us a few more wonderful things to see, like apartment door bells made of brass elf-like faces, each with its tongue sticking out, and shrines on the wall encased in metal cages which were padlocked to keep them safe; angels of every size and age, some just their heads, over doors, on walls and on roofs, and elaborate and fanciful door handles and door knockers on almost every door we looked at. Most surprising of all, though, is the number of times you see George slaying the dragon. I had always thought of St George as an English saint, but in fact it turns out he is one of the most venerated saints in the Catholic, Anglican, Eastern Orthodox and Oriental Orthodox churches. What a man!

Getting lost in Venice isn't the least bit worrying because first it's so small that you're bound to find something you recognise sooner or later, and second it's all beautiful and interesting. The bridges and calles are so clearly marked that, as long as you know which side of the Grand Canal you're on, you can easily find yourself on the most simple map.

* * * * *

After a reviving snack of peccorino, grapes and white wine, we both quite felt like going out again into the warm evening, and tonight seemed like the perfect time for us to do something we'd both secretly wanted to do right from the start; the only reason we hadn't was because we both felt a bit shy about pursuing what really doesn't fit into the cultural experience that is Venice. The thing is that both Sprat and I are huge fans of Donna Leon whose books are all set in Venice and whose hero, Guido Brunetti, is the man we both secretly want to meet and then have dinner with, at the very least. Being in Venice and actually recognising some of the places we've read about in these brilliant novels was quite exciting and great fun, so this evening we thought it was time to find the Arsenale and the via Garibaldi, both of which had been mentioned in the latest book we'd shared.

We set off in a completely new direction, down streets we had never been in before, heading vaguely north-east having found both of our goals on the map before we set out. We didn't see another tourist until we got close to the entrance of the Arsenale, and then there were only one or two explorers with cameras round their necks and guide books open. I had presumed *arsenale* would be something to do with munitions, but in fact it is, or was, a shipyard; for a long time it was the greatest and most productive naval shipyard in the world. The word 'arsenale' comes from the Arabic *darsina'a* which means house of industry, and by all accounts there couldn't have been a more accurate description for the Arsenale from the 12th Century when it was founded, right up to the 17th Century when the decline of Venice had truly set in. At the height of its powers, the Arsenale was capable of turning out an entire galley in 24 hours.

Guarding the elaborate entrance to the arsenale are two enormous lions, one sitting upright and looking forward, one lying down and staring off to its left. We wondered about the informality of these guards – usually lions like these are a matched pair and they lend an air of dignity and intimidation to the proceedings – but these two look as though they're on a break rather than on duty. The answer to this riddle is that the lions were pillaged from Piraeus near Athens in 1687 where presumably they had a more decorative role. The winged lion of Venice – the traditional symbol of St Mark – stands over the huge, elaborately carved door as it does over many doors in Venice.

The Arsenale is surrounded by crenellated walls and the entrance is guarded by two 16th century towers, one on either side of the canal. The vast complex within is under military administration and is all but abandoned and mostly closed to the public, but some parts are used as performance and exhibition spaces, especially for the Biennale. We got our first of two unexpected cultural treats from this famous exhibition. From the foot of the further tower, for almost its entire height, was what looked like an enormous red cable that had sort of frayed in places all the way up. This 'cable' was attached to the tower and then it stretched across the canal to the other tower where it was anchored in the same way. Just like the Kapoor exhibit which we saw later, it took us a while to figure out that it was a piece of art and not a dangerously neglected high voltage cable, but for all our searching we couldn't find any sort of sign telling us what we were looking at.

Leaving the Arsenale behind us we took the only route available to us and headed towards the lagoon. This stretch of promenade is called Riva dei Sette Martin and at the corner of it and the street we had just come down is the Museo Storico Navale - the Naval History Museum. It is housed on the waterfront in what used to be a warehouse and at the entrance of the museum is the most enormous anchor we've ever seen. Children were climbing on it, and one little girl, about ten years old, was only about half as tall as the prong on the side of the anchor. When we showed Mum our photos on our return, she looked carefully at this enormous anchor and said

'Is that a real child?'

We laughed so hard but actually it was quite a reasonable question if you had thought, as Mum obviously had, that the anchor might be a normal sized anchor!

We would have gone into the museum except we really wanted to keep going to find Via Garibaldi before it got too dark. Lights were beginning to come on even though it was only just dusk and we had no idea whether we were close or not, so we carried on. At the corner of the next street we found an antique shop which neither of us could resist, obviously, so we stopped and had a poke about and decided to ask the proprietor where the via Garibaldi was. He looked at us as though he was waiting for the punchline, and when he realised we weren't trying to be funny he pointed to the wall opposite and said

'Er.... here.'

We looked where he was pointing and sure enough, on the wall was the sign we'd been looking for. We'd made it.

* * * * *

The first thing we noticed about the famous street was how wide it is, and this is because, we discovered later, Napoleon made it by filling in a canal. It must have been a wide canal with a walkway on both sides of it because it's wider than any other street we'd seen in Venice so far. We wandered down the middle of it looking for Adrianna's father's shop and also for the bank from where Brunetti had followed someone. We found both and there's something oddly exciting about finding a place you've read about or even seen in the movies, like Johnny Depp's The Tourist, and finding that it really exists just as it was described, or looks exactly the same in real life as it does in a film. Adrianna's distinctive work filled her father's shop and we could easily see why they ran such a successful enterprise.

In a strange way the via Garibaldi seemed to combine old and new more than any other street in Venice. I think it might be because it's so wide which is so untypical of Venice and seems so modern, but then there are the little side streets down which the ornate lamps glow and the washing hangs across the street from wall to wall. High-end boutiques and little old fashioned *tabacchi e sale* shops side-by-side, and some distance down, the tables and umbrellas of a bar that were just waiting for us to join them. We were served very inexpensive and very nice wine by a couple of Asian lads, both yelling the odds in Italian. We sat at our table in the middle of the street watching the place coming to life with the evening crowd. People walking their dogs, families with small children out for an evening stroll and perhaps an ice cream, some shops closing and some staying optimistically open. Even after the sun had long gone the air was warm and we sat quietly and happily, sipping our excellent wine. All around us were Italian families and we weren't aware of anyone besides ourselves who wasn't speaking Italian. As long as we kept our conversation low, nobody would ever know we weren't locals. After two glasses we decided we'd better go home and get something to eat. We walked along beside the sea all the way to our familiar side street rather than trying to retrace our steps past the Arsenale and home, and we made it in no time at all. It's lucky that neither of us tires of pasta or cold meat and cheese and fruit.

~ 5 ~

Over coffee and brioche in the warm sunshine the next morning, I agreed to give up my torture-table bed and let Sprat have a go. We had tried to find a shop that sold pillows at least, and having failed at that, I decided there was nothing else to be done but suck it up and get on, or accept Sprat's offer to swap; I did the latter and looked forward to a good night's sleep.

Another gorgeous day and it seemed the perfect one for a ride across the laguna to San Giorgio. We bought some food for supper, did a little more shopping –mostly for other people, of course – and after another perfect bar lunch we set out for the bus stop. For once the *vaporetto* wasn't too crowded, and we zipped across to the island without incident. The bus stop is right in front of the church, and just as Adrianna had predicted, there were so few people that we could just wander across the forecourt to the front doors, admiring everything around us as we went. Outside the door of the church was a big notice saying that Anish Kapoor had an exhibit in the church. Sprat was delighted and excited to see it, and I was curious. Every year Venice is the venue for many and varied exhibitions and artistic events, and this piece was part of the *biennale* – the worlds largest contemporary art exhibition, held on odd-numbered years. By chance we were there on the right year, and just two days before it would close. Brilliant timing.

The interior of San Giorgio Maggiore is elegant and serene, and far into the body of it, up near the altar, was a huge, white, round, drum-like structure. We had to go up on our tiptoes to look into the middle of it, which had a large hole in it from which came a plume of steam-like vapour. The vapour swirled round and round over the hole and we couldn't really decide what the purpose of it was.

'Is this the Anish Kapoor exhibit do you think?'

'I don't know' I replied. 'If it is I have no idea what it's all about, do you?'

'Hmmm' said Sprat, as we walked around the

structure looking for some indication of what it was.

'Maybe it's a giant sort of vaporiser to keep the paintings at a constant temperature in the summer' I guessed.

We continued wandering through the church, overawed by the beauty of it all, including the two enormous Tintorettos in the chancel. Following signs to the lift, we found ourselves standing in front of a huge iron angel that looked as though it had just been put in a side corridor until somewhere more suitable could be found for it. Beside it was a stand full of postcards, so Sprat chose a few and we agreed that she would pay for them at the desk ahead of us which I presumed was the guard for the lift if it ever got busy.

Sprat showed her postcards to the two men sitting at the desk and after a brief confab, one of them waved his hand as if to dismiss the cards and said

'Niente, niente!'

Rather surprised Sprat said thank you and put the cards in her bag, and then we asked to go in the lift.

'Cinque - five - euros' said the man in the uniform.

'I thought it was free' I said in an aside to Sprat.

'Me too. Obviously things have changed.'

Turning back to the man at the desk, Sprat asked

'Where is the Anish Kapoor exhibit?'

He looked at her as though she was speaking in tongues while he computed her question and in the most bewildered tone said

'It is there - in the church!' He may as well have added 'you silly women!' because he was certainly thinking it.

'Oh!' Says I, 'we did wonder...'

Adrianna was right. There were only four other people in the tower besides us, and the views were breathtaking. Straight in front of us, across the stretch of water we'd just crossed, we could see St Mark's square, the campanile, the Doge's Palace, the Zecca and the royal gardens, glowing in the sun and reflected in the dark blue water. Behind them the brown tile roofs of Venice, the domes and towers of churches and behind that the sea and sky meeting in a rich blue backdrop for the city. On the water of the lagoon below us, boats of all sizes traveled to and fro; private and commercial, big and small, fast and slow, bright white insects on a blue carpet. Turning to the south, the land divides the water into the Grand Canal and the Giudecca Canal, over which preside the two beautiful angels and the figure of a man - perhaps San Georgio Maggiore - who stand on the top of the church's temple front. Immediately below us now, and on the land of San Giorgio Maggiore island itself, are the cloisters and gardens of what was originally a Benedictine monastery, rebuilt in the 13th Century after an earthquake. The monastery and its gardens – and an exquisite maze – are beautifully maintained and are now a thriving centre of Venetian culture of both art and theatre. The strip of land that is the island of Giudecca is divided from San Giorgio by a narrow channel of water, which takes you out to the outer islands of the lagoon. I had no idea that there were so many islands; I always thought the Venice 'experience' consisted of Venice and one or two other islands like Murano and San Giorgio, but the view from San Giorgio makes it clear that I'm wrong. Through the eastern arches of the tower is a clear view out into the lagoon and the end of Venezia. The water 'roads' are easy to make out from up high with their huge pole structures controlling the traffic as it comes and goes. And as you move from window to window and back to where you started looking at St Mark's, it seems as though you can see the whole of the coastline of Venice from east to west. By the time we had turned the 360 degrees once and taken countless photos, people had begun coming up in the lift and now we were a huge crowd of about ten, so Sprat and I decided it was time to go back down and explore the island a bit more. To our amazement, when we got into the body of the church, a plume of vapour was rising from the Kapoor exhibit. We stood and watched as it gently undulated its way up almost to the ceiling of the nave where it was sucked into a huge metal vent which had been brought into the church from outside, over the balcony railings to rest directly above the hole in the barrel of the exhibit. As we stood and watched the sensuous movement of the vapour, we realised that the four huge columns of fans positioned at equal distance round the barrel were working together with the extractor vent above to make this wonderful vortex of vapour rise up and disappear. This made perfect sense of the exhibit's title - Ascension.

* * * * *

Once outside the church we turned away from the cloisters and walked along the water's edge. The length of the walkway is a marina in which were moored big, expensive looking, beautiful yachts. On our land side we were walking beside perfectly maintained gardens and buildings, presumably all part of the cultural centre, and when we got to the end of the promenade we turned back.

Note to Self: *If a Venetian recommends something for you to do, do it!*

It was still quite early when we got back to Venice, so on our way home we decided to pretend we were tourists for a change, and join the masses for a drink at one of the enormous, impersonal, outside bars on the *riva*. We chose a table at the edge of one of these establishments and were quite quickly served by a rather attractive lady for whom this was clearly a job and not a profession. When in Venice.... so we ordered a Bellini, and shouldn't have been a bit surprised when the seconded waiter returned with a tray on which were two unopened bottles and two flute glasses. He whipped the lids off for us and poured our drinks and raced off again.

'Salute!'

'Salute!' clink, clink.

After a second sip Sprat said

'So? What do you think?'

'Hmm - sweeter than I like normally, but ok. You?'

'Probably the worst Bellini I've ever had actually, but hey, never mind, we're in Venice!'

It was lovely sitting watching the world go by, sipping our once-is-enough drinks. We decided that a drink at the bar on the way home would be a better idea and we got up and left the white cloths and bored servers behind us. At the little calle where we turned off to leave the *riva* there was a collection of gift shops and one rather nice glass shop. In it I found, at last, the perfect scent bottle for my scent-bottle-collecting sister – really made on Murano, the label said so – and then we went into the gift shop for some little stocking stuffer/grandchildren items. We both ended up buying a selection of glass lumps about the size of walnuts, made with clear glass and millefiore. When we were on Murano we had asked what they were and how they were made, and were told that when the glass blowers were at the end of their day, they would use up any little amounts of left over glass, stick some millefiore to the lump and melt them all together.

A short walk down the alley brought us out to our bar where we stopped and treated ourselves to a glass of prosecco. I suppose we had thought of prosecco the way we think of champagne at home; special occasions and only by the bottle. Now we found that you can have a glass of prosecco the same way you have a glass of ordinary vino and what a wonderful, if rather late in the day, discovery this was. While we sat in the gathering dusk watching the residents of the campo coming home after a long day or going out all dressed up for the evening, we struck up a conversation with an English couple at the next table. They were having a week in Venice – her choice – and a week in Rome – his choice – as their first holiday together for many many years. Such is the life of a farmer. When they found out where we were staying they started bombarding us with questions about how we found the flat, where we ate, how much it cost etc. and by the end of the second round of drinks they had agreed between themselves that the next time they went anywhere in Europe on holiday they would find a flat and be completely independent. It really struck a chord with them and I hope they do it because I'm sure they'd love it.

The night had settled around us so we wished our new friends a good night and a *buon viaggio* to Rome the next day, and headed home for a dish of pasta and fresh pesto. For the first time all week I could look forward to going to bed without any reservations. Poor Sprat, though.

~ 6 ~

'Are you awake?'

'I am.'

'Cuppa?'

'Ooh, I'd love one, thanks.'

By the time I came back with the tea Sprat was sitting up reading, looking very comfortable in the torture chamber.

'How did you sleep?'

'Not too bad, but it is bloody uncomfortable isn't it? How did you sleep?'

'Like a good baby' I said, 'thank you for that.'

'I'm glad, no probs. So, what's the plan for today? Ca' d'Oro maybe?'

'Yes, let's.'

Sprat had read about the Ca' d'Oro being one of the finest examples of Venetian Gothic architecture which was, at last, open to the public after being closed for renovations for a long time, and the idea of plenty of gold – d'Oro – appealed to us both. We had a vague idea of how to get there; head for the Grand Canal and turn right, and with our trusty little pop-out maps we were completely confident that we would find it, no problems. After our usual lovely, leisurely breakfast we set off in the warm autumn sunshine. Quite quickly we were out of our familiar streets and discovering new things, particularly little restaurants that we wished we'd discovered sooner. At one point, away from the shops and into a much more residential and rather run down area, we walked down one alley that opened out into a square that was quite different from most of the others we'd seen. On one side was a huge square building of flats, almost derelict looking, but that doesn't mean that it was. So many of the buildings in Venice – and indeed all over Italy in my experience – look as though they're abandoned and about to fall down and then when you get inside you find they are absolutely beautifully furnished and decorated and have been lived in forever – and this may well have been the case with these flats, but I doubt it. On the second side of the square was what looked like a most enormous church The main door was huge – at least four Sprats high – and the two doors on either side only a little smaller. Above all three doors there was evidence that whatever decoration had been there had been removed, and the whole building had an air of dejection about it. It was here, though, that we saw the only cats we'd seen in Venice in the whole week we'd been there. A little cat condominium had been built up against the wall of the church, made of boxes and covered with plastic to keep it dry. There were six or seven little 'flats', each with a towel folded neatly on its floor so the residents would stay warm. I could only see one pair of eyes looking out at me, full of suspicion, and there was one cat sunbathing in the only shaft of sunlight that had managed to find its way right to the ground. There were bowls of food there too, so they were well looked after it would seem, and thank goodness for that. On the third side of the square was a building of government offices which I think had been mentioned in one of Donna Leon's books – was it the Questura, perhaps? A very smartly dressed gentleman came out of the building while we stood staring around us. Guido?! No, not nearly not good looking enough. Sigh. And on the fourth side of the square was a canal. The ubiquitous well-head was very plain and unadorned and the victim of graffiti, and there wasn't a plant to be seen. All together a very sad and neglected place, and we were eager to move on because it wasn't how Venice should feel at all. Crossing one canal a bit further on we were surprised to see five kayaks moving slowly down the canal behind three gondolas full of happy tourists. As we stood and watched the kayaks we noticed that on the left of the canal there were three mooring posts in the water painted in a mustard yellow and white twist just like a barber shop pole. With the yellow and orange of the kayaks and the dark water of the canal, it made a striking picture. The building with the handsome mooring poles was kept in immaculate condition, the plaster and brickwork were in good repair, and the marble round the doors and windows was clean and cared for. Over the canal door were the carved heads of a pair of very severe looking gentlemen, and the iron work that covered the windows and fan lights of the doors was well maintained and mostly rust free. Venice at its best, and wouldn't I love to know who was lucky enough to live there and be able to maintain their wonderful palazzo to such a high standard. Opposite this confection was what we were more used to looking at; crumbling brick, peeling plaster and dirty marble, but still beautiful in it's uniquely Venetian way.

We continued to wander along, at one point getting caught in a bottle-neck where it seemed as though people were queueing up to cross a bridge over a canal. By the time it was our turn we could see why; the bridge was built along the side of a wall with the canal seemingly disappearing under the bridge and under the building it was attached to. It was very narrow, and at the other end it turned at a ninety degree angle for the steps to go down to the street. It was unlike any other bridge we'd come across thus far, and I'm sure that's why so many of the tourists who were crossing it felt inclined to stop and look over the railing. Not a single thought for the traffic jam they were causing, it took a bit of shoving and commenting in order to get them to move along and allow everyone else a chance to get to where they had to go. I would love to have stopped and taken a photograph but being 'local' didn't allow for such touristy behaviour...

Just as we were beginning to think we would enjoy the breathing space of a campo, we arrived at one. Venice is amazing like that; twisty, narrow lanes and just when you're feeling a tiny bit lost and claustrophobic, your alley opens up into a sunny, sky filled campo, and your equilibrium is restored. Of course the focal point of the campo was the church and unusually this one was open, with people coming and going. The square was huge, and sort of divided in two with a row of low trees and planters in front of which were set out a few tables full of touristy nicknacks. There were children running around, their grandparents watching indulgently from the benches in the sun. We carried on round the trees to the other part of the square. A few people were coming and going, and then out of nowhere burst a little white terrier, running at full speed straight at the flock of pigeons milling about looking for a hand-out. As the dog approached, the pigeons took off and fluttered a few feet just off the ground and landed again. The dog raced after them, set them up again, they flew a few lazy feet and landed, and off went the little dog again, all the time without a sound, not a single bark. They got into such a rhythm that in a very short time they'd created a sort of whirling bird vortex, up, around, down, up around some more, down, and the little dog ran faster and faster in ever increasing circles, having the most wonderful time. Another dog had come into the square, but it was on a lead and couldn't join in the fun, so the incomer did the barking and our little terrier did the chasing and jumping and everyone stopped to watch. Of course the dog didn't get near to catching a pigeon - I'm always amazed at how they continue to escape with their rather nonchalant if not downright lazy attitude - but by the time we moved on, it didn't look any closer to getting tired either.

The alley that took us out of the campo led us straight to a bridge, but just before we reached it I saw the most captivating picture on the wall. It was a framed and glazed painting of the Virgin Mary with her hands together in prayer, her eyes turned heavenward. It had a rather twenties look about its style and it must have been extremely important and precious to someone because it was almost completely hidden by the iron bars of the cage in which it had been secured. The bars were solid and close together and we kept having to change places to see a bit more of the beautiful madonna. I suppose that whoever put her there was more concerned with her safety than with how much her admirers could see.

* * * * *

We had been walking through largely residential areas; little restaurants and little shops all along the way, certainly, but no big commercial areas but now we'd arrived in a bustling shopping area. Streets – pedestrian only of course, all converged in a beautiful open, sun and tree-filled square. A church on each of two of the corners, tourists and locals coming and going, stalls selling scarves and mementos and snacks and drinks. The church closest to us was pink and white and elaborate and very much alive and we wove our way through the people and set off down the Strada Nova in search of a cup of coffee. I suppose that somewhere in Venice there must be supermarkets and department stores, but we never saw one.

The shops on the Strada Nova were typical of what we'd seen in Venice; high-end merchandise beside tourist tat. Beautiful clothes we could only look at through the window and wish for; leather goods the likes of which I would love to give to everyone I know but would go bankrupt in the process; a shop of furnishing fabrics and tassels and braids; ultra modern household lamps and mirrors and tables, and then I Heart Venice shirts, postcard stands and baskets full of glass beads and keyrings. The street was wide and there were plenty of restaurants with tables outside, so once we'd turned round and headed back towards our destination, we chose a table in the sun, and kitty bought us each a frothy coffee and a little pastry fortification.

It's all too easy to sit and people watch and soak up the sun and rest your feet, so we really had to push ourselves onwards to go and see what we'd walked all this way for. We turned right down a beautiful little street with trees and a walled garden and sure enough it was there, not very obvious and much closer to the Main Street than we had expected. The entrance hall was modern and marble and behind the desk was a very smartly dressed lady who sold us our tickets and waved her hand vaguely in the direction she wanted us to take. She did tell us that only two of the three floors were open to the public which was a disappointment, but by the time we'd been round the bits that were open, we had seen enough to fill us up for the day.

We went down first, into the 15th century courtyard, which gave us a taste of what was to come. The beautiful little courtyard with its herringbone brickwork and magnificent carved staircase that runs up the outside wall to the first floor, has been lovingly restored. As expected there is a magnificent carved well-head; this one had been removed and sold by the then owner in 1846, but when Baron Franchetti rescued Ca' d'Oro from dereliction much later, he managed to retrieve the well-head and had it restored to the house. Baron Franchetti bequeathed the house to the state in 1915, and the restoration work to bring it up to today's high standards has been going on since the 1970s.

The floor under the covered part of the courtyard is a huge, intricate mosaic of stone and marble and the walls are made of a perfectly symmetrical pattern of carved marble and terracotta. Evidence of the best materials and craftsmen of the time is everywhere, and the beautifully carved and gilded wooden virgin and baby are no less wonderful for their woodworm holes. On the first floor you're greeted by Mantegna's St Sebastian which is housed in its own alcove apart from the rest of the exhibition. The ceiling is intricately carved and gilded and it's obvious that this was a – if not the – favourite work of Baron Franchetti. The gallery opens onto the Grand Canal and is filled with the most fabulous paintings and sculpture collected by Franchetti. Sensibly there are explanatory cards in each room for which I was very grateful. It is beautifully displayed and it was the most wonderful, if slightly overwhelming way to spend the morning.

* * * * *

On our way to the Ca d'Oro we had seen a sign for the famous *traghetto* and this was the perfect opportunity for our affordable gondola ride. We joined a queue of about ten other people. Very soon after our arrival the gondola arrived and disgorged its passengers and it was our turn. We paid our few cents to the gondolier and stepped on board. I was expecting everyone to stand as is the tradition, but the first people on sat down and everyone followed suit. I wasn't about to make a fool of myself by standing and being the only one to fall overboard, so I sat too which was, of course, the right thing to do because apart from being safer, it meant I could take a picture of Sprat with the gondolier in the background, stripy jersey and aviator sunglasses filling the frame. It was really fun crossing the grand canal and I thought, secretly, that I might just save and save so that next time we go we can be ripped off like everyone else and have a little ride round the canals. I really would love to do it, just once.

The traghetto dropped us at the S.ta Sophia stop at the fish market but because we were well into the afternoon by now, everyone had gone home and the market had closed. The traghetto stop had its name beautifully painted on a sign along with the logo of the Italian menswear company, Paul and Shark. Quite appropriate outside the fish market, we thought. We both acknowledged that not only were we quite far from home, but we were also quite tired from all the walking and decided we'd take the vaporetto home. We let the first one go once it eventually arrived because it seemed to be packed to the gunwales and we didn't fancy it. A fairly long wait later another bus came along, and to our dismay we saw it was equally jam packed. However, we wanted to get home, so it was either wait ages for another one, or risk our lives on this one. Reasoning that Venetians travel this way all the time and neither of us had ever read of the vaparetto sinking in the Grand Canal, we decided to risk it. We squeezed on and wiggled our way as close to the wheel house as we could. The captain – in his aviator glasses – pulled his little window open and shouted something to the conductor and I understood enough to know that he'd been told to stop loading, the boat was full enough. A few more people pushed their way on board before the gate was closed and by now Sprat and I could barely see each other we were so crammed in. I craned round the shoulder of the man squishing me into the structure behind me and caught sight of Sprat's face. All I could think of to say for both of our sakes was 'They do it all the time - right?'

We weren't really aware of the bus leaving the dock but we were well aware of it pulling into the next stop to let three people off and twice as many on. This happened all the way down the canal and round to S Zaccaria where we had to get off, pushing and shoving and calling 'Scusi! as loudly and locally as possible, and eventually we both tumbled onto the dock, relieved to be alive and reunited.

'Wow! that wasn't much fun! You ok?'

'I am' said Sprat, 'but only because we're on

dry land and away from the very smelly lady in front of me.'

With that, and with relief, we fell about laughing and set off for home.

Because it was too early for supper but was still a beautiful evening, we decided we would go down to the campo for a drink. There's nothing like a glass of chilled prosecco, a balmy evening and good company in Italy to refresh a person, and all too soon it was time to haul ourselves back onto our feet, slowly wander the short distance home and make some supper.

Note to self: *Next time rent a flat with either a balcony or a little garden so after a long day out you can stay at home and have your drink outside without having to walk anywhere and pay someone else for it.*

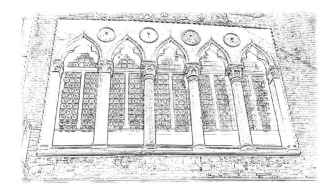

~ 7 ~

Our last day in Venice dawned bright and sunny as had every morning, actually, and by now I had got the routine of opening the window and opening the shutters and looking up to see the colour of the sky and whether there were shafts of sunlight on the roofs opposite. Venice is very tightly packed and so not a single sunbeam can find its way into many of the buildings. This is, I suppose, why there are so many campos all over the town, so everyone has a chance to sit and soak up some sun.

After breakfast - in the sun - we stayed and bought the bulk of our consumable gifts from our lovely little coffee bar. Packets of amaretto biscuits wrapped in beautifully decorated papers; slabs of nougat, little packets of caramel sticks covered in chocolate - all of which we staggered home with, rather dreading trying to pack them. We had agreed, that this being our first time in Venice we would rather indulge everyone who had to stay at home, but that we'd warn them that this would not be repeated every time we went somewhere foreign and delicious.

The only thing we really had to do was get our bus ticket to the airport for the following morning. We'd decided that this time we'd go up the Grand Canal to the airport, and see the top end of Venice that we hadn't been to. We enquired at our local ticket booth about tickets and times to the airport and were directed to the San Marco Vallaressa, straight along the Riva degli Schiavoni and just past San Marco, apparently. It was a beautiful walk and of course we discovered new places. The Zecca, only just past the columns of San Marco and San Teodoro, is a magnificent building that was the city mint until 1870. Under the trees of the Giardinetti Reali - Royal Gardens - right next to the Zecca, the rows of vendors selling mementos were still full of merchandise even this late in the season. I couldn't resist a purple t-shirt with *Ciao, Bella!* emblazoned across it in gold for my granddaughter; after all, I was outside Castello so

I was allowed to behave like a tourist, surely!

We had to queue for longer than usual to get our tickets, but as we both love people-watching and are never short of anything to say, queueing is never a hardship. Apparently we would catch the bus the next morning at S. Zaccaria and it would take us up the Grand Canal to the airport instead of taking us all the way round the island as it had when we arrived. We wandered back along under the trees and stopped to look at some of the wonderful art for sale. We were both drawn to a stall selling etchings and neither of us could resist the offer the artist made us; he was closing the next day because it was the end of his season, so he sold us each one of his most beautiful etchings for a good knock-down price. He was such a charming man too and proud to be able to tell us that his daughter is in London and he'll come to visit her now that the season has finished.

We turned away from the water and headed for one last time into St Marks's square. It was heaving with people and we were glad to just make it from one end to the other and out again, in search of some lunch. We came out of the square and because the streets in Venice move, we found ourselves in a new place, walking alongside a canal we didn't recognise, passing shops we hadn't seen before. So thrilling and so unalarming! We stood for ages looking in at the display of costumes that people can rent for Carnival and wondered who we'd dress up as when we come back for carnival sometime. When we had found the restaurant we wanted to eat at with its table all along the side of the canal, a young waitress rushed over and asked if we wanted lunch to which we said yes, but we'd be happy to wait for a table. She looked up and down and set upon a young lady who had a table to herself and who had obviously finished lunch and was now doing her studying. Our waitress was having none of it and had her packed up and moved on before we'd really figured out what was happening. No complaints from us and a good tip for her, obviously.

All the way home we picked up little last minute things, some for us and some for presents. The best thing about shopping like this is that when you get home and unwrap it all ready for packing, you find all manner of treats and treasures that you'd forgotten about. The best bit is to find you've doubled up on something so that means one for you and one for a gift - bonus!

After a little siesta to let our pannini and wine digest, we decided we'd better start the packing nightmare. We had a special outing planned for our last night and didn't want to have to hurry home and pack before we collapsed with exhaustion. At this point a little trumpet blowing ensues. I haven't learned much in my life, but one thing I do know is that statistically a person will only wear half - if that - of the clothes they take with them on holiday. Therefore it stands to reason that you need only take half of what you put out on the bed to pack because otherwise half of it will come home unworn. So, with this in mind, I'm now really good at being completely disciplined and I pack what I think isn't nearly enough but what actually turns out to be plenty. This means that I have stacks of room for packing presents. Sprat's education in this department continues, but this is only because she dresses better than I do. The result of this is that I threw everything into my bag without much trouble but Sprat had to get me to sit on her case to zip it up. It was then that the faux crocodile skin bag that she'd been bullied into buying by one of the probably illegal but very handsome and persuasive Seneglese vendors, came into its own. Into it went all the amaretti biscuits and pasta and all other crushable delights, and Sprat then carried it on the plane as hand luggage. Smart girl beating the packing crisis!

Once we were packed and before we were ready to clean out the fridge for an early supper, we went down to the bar for one last early evening drink. It was lovely to sit and watch life in the square that we had come to know quite well, and this evening was no exception. Gathering one by one and forming into small groups were children with their parents or with their older siblings, all dressed up in Halloween costumes. It hadn't even occurred to either of us that it was Halloween and now we decided to wait and see what was going to happen. A table was being set up to our right, with table cloths and plates and all sorts of food and drinks. Three or four of the children were calling up to the balcony of the flat behind us and we were amazed to hear them shouting in English with an American accent. Looking behind us we saw the mother of the children, who we both thought was obviously Italian – very beautiful with long dark hair – and then the father came out onto the balcony and discussed who had arrived for the party, if the table was laid, send your brother up here please, and so on. So all the little groups of parents and costumed children had arrived for a proper American-style halloween party. We tried to imagine how you would go Trick or Treat-ing in Venice when everyone lives in flats with one door for all.

We had the most delicious supper of pasta and cold meat and cheese and fruit, leaving just enough to make some ciabatta pannini to eat at the airport the next day. And then we set off for our big treat; we'd bought tickets to a Vivaldi concert to be played at La Pieta. Every day that we'd walked along the quayside we'd looked at the posters announcing the upcoming concerts and we'd finally decided on a treat for our last night. The history of La Pieta – or Santa Maria della Visitazione – is a wonderful story. Originally it was a foundling home for orphans and it became so popular that people would leave their children on the steps with a view to passing them off as orphans. Eventually a plaque, which is still there, was put up on the wall, threatening damnation to any parents who did this. Later Vivaldi directed the musical groups and wrote numerous pieces for the Pieta choir and the church became famous for its performances. It is still a popular venue for concerts with a strong emphasis on the music of Vivaldi. We had come to listen to a string quintet and were pleased it was all so informal and relaxed. The music was wonderful, and I looked around at the interior of this elegant church while I listened, and thought how unadorned and beautiful it was. I suppose any church after St Mark's would seem unadorned. And then the unimaginable happened, right at the end of the concert. Sprat and I got the giggles. Not just a titter, soon passed and forgotten, but full blown can't-breathe-for-laughing giggles. It was like being at school again. We got through the applause and the encores and we even managed to leave with an impression of calm but once we were outside, the end came and I was in real danger of embarrassing myself in the worst way. I was conscious of being so relieved that there was no one there that we knew to witness our hysterics. It is the best medicine though.

As we pulled ourselves together we became aware of people dressed in costume milling around us. This was enough to make us pay attention, and sure enough, people dressed in everything from witch hats and blue hair and devils with feather boas, to immaculately dressed vampires and even the phantom of the opera, were streaming past us. I decided to get some photos and pointed my camera at a handsome vampire, with white bats on his black cape, who immediately set upon Sprat, put his arm round her shoulder and grinned wickedly. Once he and his party moved on, we saw where they had all come from. Moored right up to the quayside were two wooden ships which had brought all the revellers from who knows where for a big party in Venice. I imagine it was in St Mark's and that it would have been great fun, but we hadn't come prepared and were ready to go home. A little drink on the way was a welcome idea so turning away from the party goers, we headed back to our bar and found to our dismay that it was closed. This was not good. We had finished our wine at supper so there wasn't anything at home for us.

Just out of the campo and round the corner was a little *botega* which we hadn't frequented because it had looked just a tiny bit rough for two genteel Venetian ladies... but needs must so we decided to go and brave it. Shock! horror! it too was closed! Trying not to get too excited about this turn of events, we looked down the street and saw to our delight that the lights were on and customers sitting outside the little pizza shop at the end of our *calle*. The proprietor was standing outside looking just a little agitated so we approached and asked if he was open.

'What do you want?'

'Just hot chocolate if possible, please' said Sprat.

He hesitated, looked from us to the couple still sitting at the table with the last of the bottle they were drinking and he made a decision.

'Mina!' he shouted, 'Two hot chocolate! Quickly now!'

'Oh, thank you so much!' we gushed, genuinely relieved and delighted in fact, and sat at one of the tables. Our hot chocolate arrived and it was simply delicious. While we were sipping it I could see the proprietor shuffling from one foot to the other, obviously anxious not to be here any longer.

'What's Mina doing?' I asked Sprat who had the view of the other direction.

'Having a drink!' she said.
A perfect finish to our day.

~ 8 ~

One last night in the big comfy bed for me, one last night on the rack for Sprat, and an early start the following day. Sprat had been in touch with Marika about the keys and quite fortuitously Marika couldn't make it to the flat early in the morning so she told us just to leave the keys on the table and she would pick them up later. We had one last coffee at our little coffee bar, and set off.

Walking through the city to the bus stop was the most eerie thing. There wasn't a soul about, and it wasn't even that early. It was as though Halloween signalled the grand finale of the season and when it was over, everyone went home. Then we remembered the artist by the Royal Gardens who had said pretty much that; it was the end of the season for him and he'd go to London now to see his daughter. None of the stalls were open, none of the bars or cafes on the *riva* were open, none of the gondolas were being prepared for the day and there weren't even any street sweepers, in fact it was Venice in a way we had never seen the city, not even on the morning we got up so early and went to St Mark's.

Waiting for the bus we watched the sun rising over the lagoon, sending a glittering path of light towards us. We loaded ourselves onto the bus and enjoyed the emptiness of it and a few stops down the canal we had to get off to wait for the airport bus. When it arrived there was one couple on board already, down in the cabin. We put our cases on the deck and the captain told Sprat she had to take hers into the cabin, it was too small for the deck.

'But it's too heavy!' she protested.

'Not-a my-a problem-a, I didn't pack it!' was the answer. 'You take-a it-a down-a.' Hm, and a good morning to you too!

We struggled with it into the hold and the couple who where already in there shifted themselves round so the case could fit on the floor.

'Well, he told you!' they laughed.

It was the least friendly occurrence of our

week and we think it was because it was the end of the season, the locals were all out of good manners and customer service and they needed a rest. Perhaps in December after a month of no tourists the same captain would have been delighted to help Sprat down the stairs with her case, who knows.

We were both so glad we'd decided to take this bus to the airport. It wound slowly up the canal, stopping to pick up the occasional passenger, and we were warm and comfortable in the cabin, looking out. Eventually we realised we were in the ghetto, the part of Venice that features in all the novels I have read about medieval Venice, and which Donna Leon knows about too. It's shrouded in quite a thick layer of mystique and next time we're in Venice we've decided we'll make the journey and spend a day in the ghetto and see what we can see in just that short time. The only thing I do know for sure about it is that although the Jewish community in Venice has been reduced to around 500 people, there are still all the shops and services that cater entirely for them.

Quite soon we were out into the open water and speeding towards the airport. We checked in and then found ourselves a table near a window and Sprat unpacked what would be our last, and therefore probably the best meal, in Italy; parma ham and peccorino cheese in ciabatta. We bought a coffee each and savoured every mouthful of our lunch and couldn't help wondering when we'd get the chance for a repeat performance.

Ciao, Guido.

Ciao e grazi, Venice.

Sigh.

Printed in Great Britain
by Amazon